Arthur T. (Arthur Tappan) Pierson

A memorial Address, Commemorative of the Hon. Zachariah Chandler

Arthur T. (Arthur Tappan) Pierson

A memorial Address, Commemorative of the Hon. Zachariah Chandler

ISBN/EAN: 9783337154226

Printed in Europe, USA, Canada, Australia, Japan

Cover: Foto ©ninafisch / pixelio.de

More available books at **www.hansebooks.com**

THE DORIC PILLAR OF MICHIGAN.

A MEMORIAL ADDRESS,

COMMEMORATIVE OF

The Hon. Zachariah Chandler,

UNITED STATES SENATOR,

DELIVERED IN THE

FORT STREET PRESBYTERIAN CHURCH,

DETROIT, MICHIGAN,

THURSDAY MORNING, NOVEMBER 27, 1879.

BY

ARTHUR T. PIERSON,

PASTOR.

DETROIT:
O. S. GULLEY, BORNMAN & CO., PRINTERS, 12, 14, 16 LARNED ST. EAST.
1879.

Address.

— —

"There were giants in the earth in those days" is the simple record of the age before the flood.

There has been no age without its giants; not, perhaps, in the narrow sense of great physical stature, but in the broader sense of mental might, capacity to command and control. Such men are but few, in the most favored times, and it takes but few to give shape to human history and destiny. Their words shake the world; their deeds move and mould humanity; and, as Carlyle has suggested, history is but their lengthened shadows, the indefinite prolonging of their influence even after they are dead.

One of these giants has recently fallen, at the commanding signal of one, who is far greater than any of the sons of men, and, at whose touch, kings drop their sceptre and, like the meanest of their slaves, crumble to dust.

This giant fell among us. We had seen him as he grew to his great stature and rose to his throne of power. He moved in our streets, he spoke in our halls; in our city of the living, was his earthly home.

and in our city of the dead, is his place of rest. He
went from us to the nation's capital, to represent our
State in the Senate of the Republic; he belonged to
Michigan, and Michigan gave him to the Union; but
he never forgot the home of his manhood. Here his
dearest interests clustered, and his deepest affections
gathered; and here his most loving memorial will be
reared. As he belonged peculiarly to this congrega-
tion, surely it is our privilege to weave the first wreath
to garland his memory.

The annual Day of Thanksgiving is peculiarly a
national day, since it is the only one in the year, when
the whole nation is called upon by its chief magistrate
to give thanks as a united people. By common con-
sent, it is admitted proper that, on that day, special
mention be made of matters that affect our civil and
political well-being. There is therefore an eminent
fitness in a formal commemoration, upon this day, of
the life and labors of our departed Senator and statesman.

With diffidence I attempt the task that falls to me.
The time is too short to admit even a brief sketch of a
life so long in deeds, so eventful in all that makes
material for biography: a life full, not only of inci-
dents, but of crises; moreover I am neither a senator
nor a statesman, and feel incompetent to review a
career which only the keen eye of one versed in affairs

of state can apprehend or appreciate in its full signifi-
cance; but, if you will indulge me, I will, without
conscious partiality or partisanship, calmly give utterance to the unspoken verdict of the common people,
as to our departed fellow-citizen; and try to hint at
least a few of the lessons of a life that suggests some
of the secrets of success.

History is the most profitable of all studies, and
biography is the key of history. In the lives of men,
philosophy teaches us by examples. In the analysis
of character, we detect the essential elements of success
and discern the causes of failure. Virtue and vice
impress us most in concrete forms; and hence even
the best of all books enshrines, as its priceless jewel,
the story of the only perfect life.

To draw even the profile of Mr. Chandler's public
career the proper limits of this address do not allow.
There is material, in the twenty years of his senatorial
life, which could be spread through volumes. His
advocacy of the great northwest, whose champion he
was; his master-influence, first as a member, and then
as the chairman of the committee of commerce; his
bold, keen dissection of the Harper's Ferry panic; his
sagacious organization of the presidential contests; his
plain declarations of loyalty to the Union as something which must be maintained at cost both of treasure and of blood; his large practical faculty for admin-

istration, made so conspicuous during stormy times;
his efficiency as a member of the standing committee
on the conduct of the war; his exposure of those who
were responsible for its failures, and his defence of
those who promoted its successes; his marked influence
in changing not only the channel of public sentiment,
but the current of events; his watchful guardianship
of popular interests, political and financial; his intelli-
gence and activity in senatorial debates; his attentive
and persistent study of the problem of reconstruction;
and his fearless resistance to all southern aggression
and intimidation, are among the salient points of that
long and eventful public service, whose scope is too
wide to allow at this hour even a hasty survey.

But, happily it is quite needless that in such a
presence, I should trace in detail the events of his life:
to us he was no stranger; and the mark he has made
upon our memory and our history is too deep not to
last.   His foot prints are not left upon treacherous
and shifting quicksands; and no wave of oblivion is
likely soon to wash them away.

Zachariah Chandler had nearly completed his sixty-
sixth year; forty-six years he had been a resident of
the City of the Straits.   New Hampshire was the
State of his nativity; Michigan was, in an emphatic
sense, the State of his adoption.   In our city his first
success was won in mercantile pursuits, where also

was the first field for the exhibition of his energy, ability and integrity. Here, as this century passed its meridian hour, he passed the great turning-point in his career; and his large capacities and energies were diverted into a political channel. First, mayor of the city, then nominated for governor; when, more than twenty years ago, a successor was sought for Lewis Cass, in the Senate, this already marked man became the first representative of the Republican party of this State, in that august body at Washington. There, for a period of eighteen years, he sat among the mightiest men of the nation, steadily moving toward the acknowledged leadership of his party, and the inevitable command of public affairs. After three terms in the Senate, his seat was occupied for a short time by another; but, upon the resignation of Mr. Christiancy, he was, with no little enthusiasm, re-elected, and was in the midst of a fourth term, when suddenly he was no more numbered among the living. It may be doubted whether, at this time, any one man, from Maine to Mexico, swayed the popular mind and will with a more potent sceptre than did he; and many confidently believe and affirm that, had Death spared him, he would have been lifted by the omnipotent voice and vote of the people, to the Presidency of the Republic.

Mr. Chandler took his seat in the Senate in those

days of strife when the storm was gathering, which, on the memorable 27th of April, 1861, burst upon our heads, in the first gun fired at Fort Sumpter. He entered the Senate chamber, to take the oath of office, in company with some whose names are now either famous or infamous, for all time. On the one hand, there was Jefferson Davis; on the other Hannibal Hamlin, Charles Sumner, Benjamin F. Wade and Simon Cameron.

Those were days when history is made fast. Every day throbbed with big issues. Kansas was a battle ground of freedom; and the awful struggle between State Sovereignty and National Unity was gathering, like a volcano, for its terrible outbreak. The Republican Senator from Michigan took in, at a glance, the situation of affairs. Devoted as he was to the State, whose able advocate and zealous friend he was; earnest and persistent as he was, in promoting the commercial and industrial interests of the Lake region; he was yet too much a patriot to forget the whole country; and, as the great conflict, which Mr. Seward named "irrepressible," moved steadily on towards its crisis, he armed himself for the encounter and planted his feet upon the rock of unalterable allegiance to the Union; and from that position he never swerved.

Mr. Chandler was a zealous party-man; in the eyes

of some, he was a partisan, in the strenuous advocacy of some measures; but I believe, that when History frames her ultimate, impartial verdict, she will accord to him a candid, conscientious adherence to what he believed to be a fundamental principle, absolutely essential to our national life. He saw the South, breathing hot hate toward the North, planning and threatening to rend the Union assunder. To him it was not a question simply of liberty and slavery, of sectional prejudice, of political animosity; but a matter of life or of death. He saw the scimitar of secession, raised in the gigantic hand of War—but what was it that it was proposed to cleave in twain at one blow! A living, vital form! the body of a nation, with its one grand frame-work, its common brain and heart, its network of arteries and veins, and nerves. It was not dissection as of a corpse—it was vivisection as of a corpus—that sharp blade, if it fell, would cut through a living form, and leave two quivering, bleeding parts, instead. Divide the nation! Why the same mountain ranges run down our eastern and western shores; the same great rivers, which are the arteries of our commerce, flow through both sections. Our republic is a unit by the decree of nature, that marked our nation's area and arena by the lines of territorial unity, a unit by the decree of history that records one series of common experiences; and, aside from the decree of nature and of history, it is one by the decree of necessity, for we could not survive the separation. Those were the decisive days, and they showed whose heart was yearning toward the child; and God said, as He saw a unanimous North, pleading with Him to arrest the falling sword and spare the living body of a nation's life — "give her the child for she is the mother thereof!"

Mr. Chandler has been charged with violent and even vindictive feeling toward what he deemed disloyalty and treason.

You have heard the story of the Russians, chased by a hungry pack of wolves, driving at the height of speed over the crisp snow, finding the beasts of prey gaining fast upon them; and throwing out one living child after another, to appease the maw of wolfish hunger, while the rest of the family hurried on toward safety.

There are sagacious statesmen that have declared, for a quarter of a century, that state-rights represents the pack of wolves and the sovereignty of the Union, the imperilled household. For scores of years, the encroachments of the South became more and more imperious and alarming.

Concession after concession was made, offering after offering flung to the sacrifice, but only to be followed by a hungrier clamor and demand for more;

11

and, at last, even men of peace said, "we must stop right here and fight these wolves;" and, when it becomes a question of life and death, men become desperate.

I have never supposed myself to be a strong partisan. As a man, a citizen, and a christian, I have sought to find the true political faith, and, finding it, to hold it, firmly and fearlessly. The question of the unity of our nation and the sovereignty of the national government has ever seemed to me to be of supreme moment, transcending all mere political or party issues; and, as a patriot, I cannot be indifferent to it.

When the long struggle between state-rights and national sovereignty grew hot and broke out into civil war, it was a matter of tremendous consequence that the Union be preserved. History stood pointing, with solemn finger, to the fate of the Republics of Greece and Switzerland, reminding us that confederation alone will not suffice to keep a nation alive. Mexico, at our borders, was a warning against dismemberment or the loss of the supremacy of a republican unity. And men of all parties forgot party issues in patriotic devotion. It may be a question whether state sovereignty, however fatal to national life, deserved the hideous name of treason, before the war. But, after the matter had been referred to the arbitrament of the sword, and had been settled at such cost of blood and treasure, it can never henceforth be anything but treason, again to raise that issue. Hence, even men that were temperate in their opposition to southern aggressions before the war, now are impatient. They set their teeth with the resolution of despair, and say, "we make no further effort to escape this issue, and we throw out no more offerings of concession. We shall fight these wolves; and either state-rights or national sovereignty shall die."

This was Mr. Chandler's position: if it was a mistaken one, it is the unspoken verdict of millions of the best men of all parties in the whole country; and every new concession to this great national heresy is only making new converts to the necessity of a firm and fearless resistance.

Some one has suggested that the old division of the church into militant and triumphant is no longer sufficient; we must add another, namely, the church termigant. In our country both sections were militant, and one was triumphant; the other has been very termigant ever since. General Grant, at his reception in Chicago, declared that the war for the Union had put the Republic on a new footing abroad. A quarter of a century ago, by political leaders across the sea, "it was believed we had no nation. It was merely a confederation of states, tied together by a rope of sand, and would give way upon the slightest friction. They have found it was a grand mistake. They know we have now a nation, that we are a nation of strong and intelligent and brave people, capable of judging and knowing our rights, and determined on all occasions to maintain them against either domestic or foreign foes; and that is the reception you, as a nation, have received through me while I was abroad."

On the same day we have a significant voice from the south. General Toombs, in response to a suggestion that governors of various states and prominent southern men should unite in congratulations to the ex-president on his return, telegraphs in these words: "I decline to answer except to say, I present my personal congratulations to General Grant on his safe return to his country. He fought for his country honorably and won. I fought for mine and lost. I am ready to try it over! Death to the Union!"

Here we have simply two representative utterances; one is the voice of a solid North; the other is we fear the voice of a South, that is much more "solid" than we could wish. It is no marvel if, after a war of so many years, that cost so many lives and so much money, and left us to drag through ten years of a financial slough, loyal men are impatient and even angry, when they discover that the question is still an unsettled one, and that we have not even conquered a

peace! Even the interpretation now attached to this
seditious utterance by General Toombs himself, that
"the result of the war was death to the Union, and
that the present government is a consolidated one, not
a confederacy," does not essentially relieve the matter.

Mr. Chandler could not brook what he regarded
as sentiments rendered doubly treasonable by the fact
that a long, bitter but successful war had burned upon
them with a hot iron the brand of treason. He fought
those sentiments, and it was as under a black flag that
announced "no quarter." But this does not prove
malicious or vindictive feeling toward misguided men,
who hold such views. There is a difference between
fighting a principle and fighting a person. In fact the
only way to prevent fighting men is often a vigorous
and timely opposition to their measures. And if we
wish to avoid another war and, that, a war of extermi-
nation, the ballot must obviate the necessity for the
bullet; we must stand together, and by our voice and
vote, by tongue and pen, by our laws and our acts, in
the use of every keen weapon, exterminate the heresy
of state-rights. We need not do this in hate toward
the South; a true love even for the South demands it,
for to them as to us it is a deadly foe to all true
prosperity, and national existence. How can a man
who candidly looks upon the present attitude of the
South as both suicidal and nationally destructive, be

15

calm and cool? The philippics of Demosthenes were bitter, but they were the mighty beatings of a heart that pulsed with the patriotism that could not see liberty throttled without sounding a loud and indignant alarm. The North owes a big debt to every man who at this crisis will not suffer an imperilled Republic to sleep!

Mr. Chandler was not a college-graduate. His early training was got in the New England common school and academy. Yet he was in a true sense an educated man: for education is 'not a dead mass of accumulations,' but self-development, 'power to work with the brain;' to use the hand in cunning and curious industries, to use the tongue in attractive and effective speech, to use the pen in wise, witty or weighty paragraphs. Somehow he had learned to hold, with a master hand, the reins of his own mind, and make his imagination and reason and memory and powers of speech obey his behests. That is no common acquirement: it is something beyond all mere acquirement: it is the infallible sign and seal of culture. His addresses, even on critical occasions, were unwritten, and, in some cases, could not have been elaborated, even in the mind: yet in vigor of thought, logical continuity and consistency, accuracy of diction, and even rhetorical grace, few public speakers equal them.

The power to command the popular ear is a rare power, whether it be a gift of nature or a grace of culture. With Mr. Chandler it was held and wielded as a native sceptre. He had the secret of rhetorical adaptation: he could at once go down to the level of the people and yet lift them to his level. They understood what he said, and knew what he meant. He threw himself into their modes of thought and habits of speech: he culled his illustrations mainly from common life. If he sacrificed anything, it was rhetorical elegance, never force; his one aim was to compel conviction.

The simplicity of his diction was a prime element and secret of his power. He did not speak as one who had to say something, but as one who had something to say, and whose whole aim was to say it well; with clearness, plainness, force and effect. If he could not have both weight and lustre, he would have weight.

Walter Scott has exposed the absurdity of 'writing down' to children, and shown that it is really writing up, to make oneself so simple as to be plain even to the child-mind. Simplicity is the highest art. To have thought faintly gloom and glimmer through obscure language, like stars through a haze or mist, may serve to impress the ignorant with a supposed profundity in the speaker; but it is no more a sign of such profundity than muddy water signifies depth in a stream; it may suggest depth because you can see no bottom, but it means shallowness! It is a lesson that all of us may well learn from the life of our departed senator, that the first element of good speaking is thought; and the second a form of words fitting the thought, which, like true dress, shall not call attention to itself but to the idea or conception which it clothes. Any man who is long to hold the ear of the people must give them facts and thoughts worth knowing and thinking of, in words which it will not take a walking dictionary or living encyclopædia to interpret, or a philosopher to untangle from the skein of their confusion.

Mr. Chandler was such a man, a man for the people. Free from all stately airs and stilted dignities, he took hold of every political and national question with ungloved hands. He understood and used the language of home life, which is the 'universal dialect' of power. His speeches were packed with vigorous Saxon. He thought more of the short sword, with its sharp edge and keen point and close thrust, than of the scholar's labored latinity, with its longer blade, even though it might also have a diamond-decked hilt; and in this, as in not a few other conspicuous traits, he was master of the best secrets that gave the great Irish agitator, O'Connell, his strange power of moving the multitude. His last speech, even when read, and without the magnetism of his personal presence, may well stand as the last of his utterances.

The simplicity of Mr. Chandler's style of oratory amounted to ruggedness, in the sense in which we apply that word to the naked naturalness of a landscape, whose features have not been too much modified by art. There is in oratory an excessive polish, which suggests coldness and deadness. Some speakers sharpen the blade until there is no blade left; the mistaken carefulness of their culture brings everything to one dead level of faultlessness; there is nothing to offend, and nothing to rouse and move. Demosthenes said that kinésis—not 'action,' but motion, or rather that which moves, is the first, second, third requisite of true oratory. He is no true speaker who simply pleases you; he must stir you to new thought, new choice, new action.

We must beware of the polish that is a loss of power, and, like a lapidary, not grind off points, but grind into points. Demosthenes was more rugged than Cicero; but he pricked men more with the point of his oratorical goad. Men heard the silver-tongued Roman and said, "how pleasantly he speaks!" They heard the bold Athenian and shouted, "Let us go and fight Philip!"

Carlyle says, "he is God's anointed king whose simple word can melt a million wills into his!" That melting wills into his own is the test of eloquence in the orator: and a rugged simplicity has held men in the very fire of the orator's ardor and fervor, till they were at white heat, and could be shaped at will; while the most scholarly display of culture often leaves them unmoved, to gape and stare with wonder, as before the splendors of the Aurora Borealis, and feel as little real warmth. Emerson is right: 'there is no true eloquence unless there is a man behind the speech,' and men care not what the speech is, if the man be not behind it, or on the other hand what the speech is, if the man be behind it! And so it is that Richard Cobden compelled even Robert Peel, who loved truth and candor, to become a convert to his free-trade opinions: and so it was that John Bright, another model of a simple utterance with a sincere man behind it, swayed such a mighty sceptre over the people of Britain. The mere declaimer or demagogue may win a temporary hearing: but the man who leaves a lasting impress on the mind of the people must have in himself some real worth.

To Mr. Chandler's executive ability, reference has been made. It was never better illustrated than in his vigorous and faithful administration as Secretary of the Interior. It was Hercules in the Augean Sta-

---

bles, again—purging the department, of incompetency and dishonesty. He sent a flood through the pension bureau, that swept all the clerks out of one room; and another through the Indian bureau, that cleaned out its abuses and exposed its frauds. It is said that the reconstruction of that department saved millions annually to the treasury of the nation. Mr. Schurz, in becoming his successor, paid a very handsome tribute to the retiring Secretary, acknowledging the great debt of the country to Mr. Chandler's energy and fidelity, and modestly declaring that he could hope for no higher success than to keep and leave the department where he found it.

If there be any one thing for which the Senator from Michigan stood above most men it was in this practical business ability. He had, in rare union, 'talent' and 'tact.' His good sense, clear views, ready and retentive memory, prompt decision, patience and perseverance, quick discernment and instinctive perception of the fitness of ways to ends, qualified him for energetic and successful administration anywhere. Webster said, "there is always room at the top." Even the pyramid waits for the capstone, which must be, itself, a little pyramid. And he, who has inborn or inbred fitness for the top place, will find his way there; no other will long stay there, even if some accident lifts him to the nominal occupancy of such a position.

He had rare tact, that indefinable quality of which Ross says, that "it is the most exquisite thing in man." Literally it means 'touch,' and is suggested by the delicacy often found in that mysterious sense. It describes, though it cannot define, the nice, skilful, innate discernment and discrimination which tells one what to say and do, even on critical occasions; how to reach and 'touch' men, when a blunder would be fatal. This wisdom of instinct may be cultivated but cannot be acquired; and it seems to be close of kin with that common sense which, though by no means exceedingly 'common,' represents a sound intuitive sense in common matters, such as would be the common sense or verdict of wise and sagacious minds.

The Senator impressed men as one whose powers were varied and versatile. Thomas F. Marshall, the 'Kentucky orator,' maintained that fine speaking, writing and conversation depend on a different order of gifts. "A speech cannot be reported, nor an essay spoken. Fox wrote speeches; nobody reads them. Sir James Mackintosh spoke essays; nobody listened. Yet England crowded to hear Fox, and reads Mackintosh. Lord Bolingbroke excelled in all, the ablest orator, finest writer, most elegant drawing-room gentleman in England."

22

Whether or not this philosophy be sound and this
estimate correct, we shall all agree that few men combine power of speech with force in composition and
grace in conversation. Our departed Senator certainly
had more than the common share of versatility. That
last speech at Chicago thrilled a vast audience when
spoken, and kindled a flaming enthusiasm; yet it
reads like the compact and complete sentences of the
essayist.

Versatility, however, is not to be coveted where it
implies a lack of concentration. An anonymous
writer has left us a very discriminating comparison of
two great British statesmen. He likens Canning's
mind to a convex speculum which scattered its rays of
light upon all objects; while he likens Brougham's to
a concave speculum which concentrated the rays upon
one central, burning, focal point. There are some men
who possess, to a considerable degree, both the power
to scatter and the power to gather the rays. At times
they exhibit varied and versatile ability, they touch
delicately and skilfully many different themes or
departments of thought and action; but when crises
arise which demand the whole man, they become in
the best sense men of one idea, for one thought fills
and fires the soul; every power is concentrated in one
burning purpose.

The Senator, whose deserved garland we are weaving, was one of these men. There were times when he seemed to turn his hand with equal ease to a score of employments; now giving wise counsel in gravest matters, now playfully entertaining guests at his table; now studying the deep philosophy of political economy, now holding a senate in rapt attention; now reorganizing a department of state, now pushing a new measure through Congress; now closeted with the President over the issues of a colossal campaign, and again conducting a pleasure excursion; to-day leading on the hosts of a great party, and to-morrow managing the affairs of an extensive farm. But, when the destiny of the nation hung in the balance, or History waited with uplifted pen, to record, on her eternal scroll, the final decision of some great question, he gathered and condensed into absolute unity all the powers of mind and heart and will, and flung the combined weight of his whole manhood into the trembling scale. When he felt that a thing must be, a mountain was no obstacle to surmount, a host of foes no occasion for dismay. With intensity of conviction, with contagious courage and enthusiasm, with indomitable resolution, with tireless energy of action, he went ahead, and weaker men had to follow; his conviction persuaded the hesitating, his courage emboldened the timid, his determination inspired the irresolute. He was the unit that, in the leading place, makes even the cyphers swell the sum of power.

It is no slight praise of Mr. Chandler to say that he was a man of industry : the results he reached were won by work. There is a great deal of blind talk about genius. That there is such a thing, apart from the practical faculty of application, even great men have doubted or boldly denied ; but certain it is that there is such a thing as the genius of industry, and that rules the world ! Alexander Hamilton disclaimed any other genius than the profound study of a subject. He kept before him a theme which he meant to master, till he explored it in all its bearings and his mind was filled with it. Then, to quote his words, "the effort which I make the people are pleased to call the fruit of genius. It is the fruit of labor and thought."

And so for us all there is no royal road to a true success. We must simply plod on, along the plain, hard, plebeian path of honest toil, and climb up the hills, if we would get on and up at all. Spinoza grandly says that there is no foe or barrier to progress, like "self-conceit and the laziness which self-conceit begets." We venture to add that no conceit is surer to beget laziness than the conceit of 'conscious genius.' Our peril is to learn to do our work easily : that means poor work, if indeed any work at all, shallow acquirements, superficial attainments, and no real scholarly or heroic achievements.

Our regretted Senator did not despise honest work, and never claimed to be a genius. He had a hearty contempt for all that aristocracy of intellect that frowns on mental toil.

He spoke without manuscript, and without memorizing; or, as we say, 'extempore.' That is another much abused word. Extemporaneous speech is not the utterance of words that shake the world, or any considerable part of it, unless such speech be the fruit not of that time, but, as Dr. Shedd says, "of all time, previous." But when the orator first becomes master of his theme, and then of the occasion; and is thus fitted to deal with the real vital issues before the people; he may, without having put pen to paper, or having framed a single sentence beforehand, often find himself master also of his audience. The careful study of his subject, the habit of thinking in words, and of weighing words when he reads and talks, scoops out a channel in the mind; and when he rises to speak he finds his thought flowing naturally and easily in this channel.

No man can carefully read Mr. Chandler's public utterances without detecting a brevity and terseness, a simplicity and plainness, an accuracy and vigor, and often a rhetorical beauty, which shew care in prepara-

tion. These qualities are not the offspring of indo-
lence. Years of drill lie back of the exact and daring
touches with which the artist makes the canvas speak
and the marble breathe; and the extempore speech of
the eloquent orator tells of long, hard discipline that
has taught him how to think and how to talk: it may
have taken him fifty years, to learn how to hold and
sway an audience at will for fifty minutes. The ease
and grace of true oratory are the signs of previous
exertion; of that systematic exercise of the intellect
that has suggested for our training schools, the name,
gymnasia. The laws of brain and of brawn do not
differ much in this respect. Men are not born athe-
letes, either in mind or muscle; and to all who have
a true desire to succeed, in any sphere of life, the one
voice that, with the growing emphasis of the success-
ive centuries, speaks to us, is, "whatsoever thy hand
findeth to do, do it with thy might." Your sword
may be short; "add a step to it!" it may be dull; add
force to the blow or the thrust. There is no encour-
agement from History, more universally to be appro-
priated by us, than the testimony she furnishes to the
power and value of honest endeavor. To will and to
work is to win. The highest endowments assure no
achievements; all success is the crown of patient toil!

While thus speaking a word in favor of hard work,
one word of caution and of qualification may not be

out of place. I think God means that the sudden decease of public men when in life's prime, shall not be without warning. No thoughtful man fails to feel the force of this fact that somehow the average duration of human life, especially on these shores and among men of mark, is shortening; and that apoplexy, paralysis, angina pectoris, cerebral hemorrhage, and softening of the brain are amazingly common among brain-workers. The fatality among journalists is especially startling.

We are a fast-living and a fast-dying people. Our habits are bad. We work hard half the time and worry, the other half. We eat and sleep irregularly; we tax our powers unduly, keeping the bow bent until the string snaps simply from constant tension, lack of relaxation. We turn night into day, without restoring the balance by turning day into night. We live in an atmosphere of excitement, and push on to the verge of death before we know our peril or realize our risk. We are tempted to put stimulus in the place of strength, that we may do, under unnatural pressure, what we cannot do by nature's healthy powers. Instead of repairing the engine, we crowd fuel into the boiler and get up more steam; and, by and by, something breaks, or bursts, and the machinery is a wreck.

I believe it is not hard work that kills us, so much

as work under wrong conditions. To do, with the aid
of even mild stimulants, like tea and coffee, not to say
tobacco, opium, quinine, etc., what we cannot do by
the natural strength, is the worst kind of overwork;
and yet our public men are subject to such strain, that
they are almost driven to such resorts. Where they
ought to stop, and sleep and rest, they 'key up' with
a kind of artificial strength, and get the habit of
unnatural wakefulness; and then wonder why they
are victims of insomnia.

Prof. Tyndall, one of the most tireless men of
brain, in our day, says to the students of University
College, London: "Take care of your health! Imagine
Hercules, as oarsman in a rotten boat; what can he do
there but, by the very force of his stroke, expedite the
ruin of his craft! Take care of the timbers of your
boat!" And Dr. Beard adds: "To work hard without overworking, to work without worrying, to do
just enough without doing too much—these are the
great problems of our future. Our earlier Franklin
taught us to combine industry with economy; our
'later Franklin' taught us to combine industry with
temperance; our future Franklin—if one should arise
—must teach us how to combine industry with the
art of taking it easy."

The qualities that fitted Mr. Chandler for the conduct of affairs were, however, not purely intellectual:

they belonged in part to another and a higher order, viz: the emotions and affections.

He had great intensity of nature. Even his political opponents could not doubt the positiveness of his conviction and the profoundness of his sincerity; and here, as Carlyle justly says, must be found the base blocks in the structure of all heroic character. It is no small thing to be able to command even from antagonist the concession and confession of one's sincerity. Candor atones for a host of faults. Men will, at the last, forgive anything else in a man who tries to be true to his own convictions and to their interests. The utterances of impulse and even of passion, stinging sarcasm and biting ridicule, unjust charges and assaults, all are easy to pardon in one whose sincerity and intensity of conviction betray him into too great heat; men would rather be scorched or singed a little in the burning flame of a passionate earnestness than freeze in the atmosphere of a human iceberg—beneath whose rhetorical brilliance, they feel the chill of a cold, calculating insincerity and hypocrisy that upsets their faith in human honesty.

He was also peculiarly independent and intrepid. The determination to be loyal, both to his convictions and to his country, inspired him to a bold, brave utterance and invested him with a courage and confidence that were almost contagious. We cannot but admire

the political fidelity expressed by Burke in his famous
defence before the Electors of Bristol, when he said:
"I obeyed the instructions of nature and reason and
conscience: I maintained your interests, as against
your convictions." Few men have ever dared to say
and do what Mr. Chandler has, in the face of such
political risks and even such personal peril. One
brief address delivered by him in the Senate, soon
after he resumed his seat, will stand among the classics
of our language, and, if I may so say, among the
'heroics' of our history.

He was also a man of great political integrity. In
the long career of a public life spanning more than a
quarter of a century no suspicion of dishonesty or disloyalty has ever stained his character or reputation.
Michigan may safely challenge any senatorial record
of twenty years to surpass his, either in the quantity or
quality of public service.

Those who knew him best affirm that he was,
politically and personally an incorruptible man. The
position of a legislator is one of proverbial peril. From
the days of Pericles and Augustus till now, the men
who make laws and guide national affairs are peculiarly in danger of defiling their consciences by 'fear
or favor.' Bribery sits in the vestibule of every law-
making assembly. Greed holds out golden opportunity for getting enormous profits from unlawful or

---

questionable schemes and investments. Ambition lifts her shining crown, and offers a throne of commanding influence if you will bow down and worship, or even make some slight concession in favor of the devil. Only a little elasticity of conscience, a little blunting of the moral sense; a little falsehood or perjury or treachery, under polite names; a lending of one's name to doubtful schemes; and there is a rich reward in gains to the purse and gratifications to the pride, which more than pay for the trifling loss of self-respect. And so not a few who go to Congress with unsullied reputation, come back smutched with their participation in 'Credit Mobilier' and 'Pacific Railroad' schemes, or any one of a thousand forms of fraud.

So far as I know, Mr. Chandler has never been charged with complicity as to dishonest and disgraceful measures such as have sometimes made the very atmosphere of the capitol a stench in the nostrils of the pure and good. His name does not stand on the pay-roll of Satan, but with the honored few whose eyes have never been blinded by a bribe, and whose record has never been blotted with political dishonor.

To have simply done one's duty is no mean victory. To stand—like the anvil beneath the blows of the hammer—and firmly resist the force of a repeated temptation, is grand and heroic. To be venal is no

venial fault; no price, which can be weighed in gold,
can pay a man for the sale of one ounce of his manliness. Conscience is a Samson, whose locks are easily
shorn, but they never grow again; whose eyes, once
put out or seared with a hot iron, no prayer will
restore. And men, as great and wise as Bacon, have
like him been compelled to confess to their own mean-
ness and the mercenary character of their virtue.

One of the worst signs of the times is this corrupt-
ibility of popular leaders. One of the greatest of
European journals moves like a weather-vane just as
the day's wind blows. Much of the best talent of
Europe is for sale for or against despotism. Some of
the most gifted men in the House of Lords are of
plebeian birth, bought by the bribe of a title, as Harry
Brougham himself was, when his great influence
became a terror to the aristocracy; and the Duke of
Newcastle is said to have bought one-third of the
House of Commons. There is scarce a measure however infamous that may not be pushed through our
Common Councils, and legislative bodies, if the lobby-
ists are only 'influential and numerous,' and the money
is only plenty enough. Let us give God thanks for
every man in the community who is not on the auc-
tion block to be knocked down to the highest bidder.
In these days of abounding fraud and falsehood, men
are beginning to feel the value of simple honesty.

We have, in our admiration of the genius of intellect, forgotten the genius of goodness which has power to inspire men with heroism. Better to strengthen a few timid hearts in loyalty to principle than to have deserved the encomium of Augustus who 'found Rome, brick, and left it, marble.' The Earl of Chatham refused to keep a million pounds of government funds in the bank and pocket the proceeds; as Edmund Burke on becoming paymaster general, first of all introduced a bill for the reorganization of that department of public service, refusing to enrich himself, through the emoluments of that lucrative office, at public expense.

No wonder George the Second should have said of such 'honesty' that it is an 'honor to human nature!' Such words were worthy of a king, but it is only a crowned head bowing to royal natures that need no crown to tell that they are kingly. The distinguished Hungarian exile will never be forgiven for saying that he would praise anything and anybody to aid Hungary. There is an instinct in the great heart of humanity which not even wickedness kills, that no quality is so fundamental to character as absolute loyalty to truth; it is the base block of the whole structure; and great has been many a 'fall,' where there is no better foundation than the treacherous

5

34

and shifting quicksands of what is called 'policy,' and which is to many the only standard of honesty.

Mr. Chandler was known in politics as an enthusiastic and radical advocate of his party and its measures. It was not in him to do anything by halves; and it is difficult to see why one may not as naturally be zealous in politics as in religion; in fact none are more likely to charge upon him partizanship than those who in their attachment to the opposite party shew their own lack of moderation.

It has been well said that religion demands "a faith, a polity and a party." The faith and the polity belong to it as necessary features; the party is that on which it depends for organization and onward movement. There is a philosophy, a political creed and economy, which are, to the state, what religion is to the church; and no man can be a patriot without a political faith and polity and party; though he may stand alone, he represents all three. He may be in the largest sense a patriot, and adopt the sublime motto of Demosthenes: "Not father, nor mother, but dear native land!" yet his patriotism may compel him, as he looks at the matter of his country's interest, to take a position on the side of a political party, and to hold it in the face of ridicule and reproach and even of a pelting hail of hate. Others may not be wrong in their espousal of a different political creed,

but he is not wrong, but right, in his honest adherence
to his. It is so in religion: an honest, intelligent man
is loyal to his own denomination, yet is he none the
less, because of that, a christian, in the breadth of his
charity.

In fact religion is not the only sphere where self-
sacrifice, for duty and for conscience, may be pressed
even to martyrdom. St. Ignatius, facing the wild
beasts in the arena, calmly said, "I am grain of God;
I must be ground between teeth of lions to make
bread for God's people." That was the grand confession of a christian martyr. Tell me, how much
lower down in the scale of the heroic does he belong
who, for the sake of the best good of a constituency
blinded by passion or prejudice, like the great English
statesman, consents to be hurled from his shrine as the
idol of the people, and calmly says, "I am under no
obligation to be popular, but I am under bonds to myself to be true!" When Regulus refused to buy his
own liberty and life, at the cost of Rome's disgrace,
and persuaded the Senate to reject the very overtures
which he was commissioned to convey, himself return-
ing as his pledge required him if the negotiations were
unsuccessful, and surrendering himself to the will of
his enemies that Carthage might put him to death by
slow torture, it seems to me something like the martyr-
spirit burned in that bosom. And, if there be nothing

akin to moral martyrdom, in bravely standing in one's
place and boldly holding one's ground, advocating
what one believes to be the only true creed in politics,
and the only true policy for the country, in face of
sneer and threat, daring the blade and the bullet, the
open affront and the secret assault, for the sake of
being true to oneself and to one's native land; if there
be nothing sublime and heroic in all this, the verdict
of reason is unsound.

This lamented statesman had also a genial temper
which won for him a host of friends. Public men are
prone to one of two extremes: either the hypocritical
suavity of the demagogue, or the arbitrary bluntness
and curtness of the despot. Some swing away from
the fawning airs of the puppy, but it is toward the
repulsive manners of the bear. The man who, as you
tip your hat, with a polite good morning, sweeps by,
saying 'I haven't time,' is too often the typical man of
affairs, who thinks the quick dismission of applicants
and intruders is the price of all energetic public service. It is said of the great French statesman, Richelieu,
that he could say "no," so gracefully and winningly,
that a man once became applicant for a position upon
which he had not the least claim, just to hear the great
Cardinal refuse. If common testimony may be trusted,
Michigan's esteemed Senator seldom lost the hearty

cordiality and courtesy of his manners, even under the fretting friction of public cares.

I am tempted to add that, though a representative republican, Mr. Chandler was, in the best sense, a democrat. He weighed a man according to the worth of his manhood. He could recognize true manliness, beneath a black skin as well as a white one, and behind the rough dress of a poor man, as behind broadcloth; and, because he was the friend of humanity and of human rights, you will find some of his warmest friends among the common people and in the lower ranks.

I think both justice and generosity demand that among the tributes we weave for him, there should be distinct and emphatic mention of this simplicity of character. He was a man among men. From the first, he had none of those assumptions of conscious superiority, that mark the aristocrat. If anything, he was rather careless than careful of his dignity, and would sooner shock than mock the fastidious airs and tastes of those who prate about culture, or pride themselves on their 'nobility.' Fox quaintly said, of the elder Pitt, that he 'fell up stairs' when he was elevated to the peerage. Many a man cannot stand going up higher. He becomes haughty, proud; he affects dignity, he lords it over God's heritage, he becomes too

big with conscious superiority. Like Jeshurun, he
waxes fat and kicks. He falls upstairs, if not down.

The warm, soft, genial side of Mr. Chandler's nature was unveiled in social life and most of all in the
domestic circle. The play of his smile, the roar of
his laughter, the delicacy and tenderness of his sym-
pathy, his stalwart defense of those whom he loved;
the childlike traits that drew him to children and
drew children to him, none appreciate as do those who
knew him best as friend, husband and father. The
man of public affairs, he could lay one hand firmly on
the helm of state, while with the other he fondly
pressed his grandchildren to his bosom, or playfully
roused them to childish glee.

This aspect of his many-sided character makes his
death an irreparable loss to his own household. Even
the great grief of a nation cannot represent by its
'extensity,' the intensity of the more private sorrow
that secludes itself from the public eye. He was, to
those whom he specially loved, both a tower for
strength, and a lover and friend for comfort and sym-
pathy. Those who were 'at home' with him, and
especially those who were the peculiar treasures of
his heart, knew him as no others could. Happy is the
minister who forgets not his parish at home—the
church that is in his own house—and happy is the
public man, whose private life is not simply the reve-

lation of the hard, coarse and unattractive side of his character.

That is I am sure no ordinary occurrence, which has made forever memorable the Calends of this November. Death, however frequent and familiar by frequency, can never, to the thoughtful, be an event of common magnitude; the exchange of worlds cannot be other than a most august experience. But this death has about it colossal proportions; it stands out and apart like a mountain in a landscape. It is recognized as a calamity not only to a household, but to the city, the state, the nation; and it may be doubted whether, since the assassination of Abraham Lincoln, any single announcement has so startled the public mind and moved the popular heart as when on the first day of November it was announced that Zachariah Chandler was found sleeping his last sleep.

Ulysses S. Grant is a man of few words—and like his shot and shell they weigh a good deal and are well aimed. Let us hear his verdict on Mr. Chandler.

"A nation, as well as the State of Michigan, mourns the loss of one of her most brave, patriotic and truest citizens. Senator Chandler was beloved by his associates and respected by those who disagreed with his political views. The more closely I became

acquainted with him, the more I appreciated his great
merits."   U. S. GRANT.

Galena, Ill., Nov. 9, 1879.

It is evident that it is no ordinary man, who has
departed from among us.   It is not "a self-evident
truth that all men are created equal," if we mean
equality of gifts and graces, capacity, opportunity or
even responsibility ; and the people of these United
States do not need to be told that Mr. Chandler was
no common man.   It was by no accident that he held
in succession, and filled with success, posts of such im-
portance and trusts of such magnitude.   He did not
drift into prominence : he rose by sheer force of character and by the fitness of things.   Born to be a
leader, endowed with those qualities that mark a man
destined to leadership, having rare business faculty,
and sagacity, tact and talent ; large capacity for organization and administration ; his hand was naturally
at the helm.

Mr. Chandler's leadership reached beyond and beneath the visible conduct of affairs.   As Moses was
the inspiration, of which Aaron was the expression, he
was often the power behind the throne.   He who has
now left us, forever, belonged to the illustrious few,
who were the special counsellors of Mr. Lincoln and
the instigators of many of his wisest and best measures.   There is an inner history of the war which has

never been written and never will be. The lips that
alone could disclose those secrets are fast closing in
eternal silence, and the scroll will find no man worthy
to loose its seals.

Mr. Chandler could not have been wholly ignorant
of the risk he ran in his laborious and prolonged cam-
paign-work; but when his country seemed in peril his
tongue could not keep silence. Just before starting
on his last journey westward, he said to me: "In my
judgment the crisis now upon us is more important
than any since Lee surrendered, and as grave as any
since Sumpter was fired on." Those who knew him
best will not be surprised that, with such an impres-
sion of the magnitude of the issues now before the
American people, he could not spare himself, but gave
himself without reserve to his country, sacrificing his
life itself on the altar of his own patriotism.

And so our stalwart statesman has fallen, and we
have a new lesson on human mortality. Anaxagoras,
when told that the Athenians had condemned him to
die, calmly added, "And nature, them!" All our
riches, honors, dignities cannot stay the steps of the
great destroyer. The manliest and mightiest leaders,
and the humblest and meanest followers bow alike to
the awful mandate of death. And as Massilon said at
the funeral of the Grand Monarch, "God only is
great!"

42

Of how little consequence after all are all the
things that perish. Temporal things derive all their
true value from their connection with the invisible
and eternal. How small will all appear as they recede
into the dim distance at the dying hour and the world
to come confronts us with its awful decisions of destiny! What grandeur and glory are imparted to our
humblest sphere of service, here, when touched and
transformed by the power of an endless life!

We have reason to be glad that the popular recog-
nition of Mr. Chandler's abilities and services has been
so prompt and hearty as to afford him not a little
satisfaction. Posthumous tributes are sometimes mel-
ancholy memorials, reminding us of the monumental
sepulchres of martyr-prophets.

Robert Burns' mother said about his monument, as
she bitterly remembered how the poet of Ayr had
been left to starve, "Ah, Robbie, ye asked them for
bread and they hae gi'en ye a stane!" It can never
be said that our departed Senator had to wait for
another generation to pronounce a just or generous
verdict upon his career; the trophies of victory and
of popular esteem were strewn along the whole line
of his march; and his last tour of the Northwest was
a perpetual ovation.

There is to my mind no little inspiration of comfort in the fact that not even human malice can falsify

history. Men sometimes get more than their share of praise or of blame while they live; but sooner or later the cloud of incense or the mist of prejudice clears away and the real character is more plainly seen. We can afford to leave the final verdict to another generation if need be, grateful as it is to be appreciated by the generation which we seek to serve.

But it is still more inspiring to know that God rules this world, and reigns over the affairs of men. If He marks the flight and the fall of the sparrow, we may be sure that no man rises to the seat of power or sinks to the grave without His permission.

God is not dead, and cannot die. Generations pass away while He remains the same. His hand is on the helm, whatever human hand seems to have hold, and is still there when the most trusted helmsman relaxes his dying grasp. If God's hand is not in our history, all its records are misleading, and all its course a mystery. Admit the divine factor, and, from the strange unveiling of this hidden Western world until this day, our national life appears like one colossal crystal; it has unity, transparency and symmetry. We can understand Plymouth Rock, the Revolution, the French and Indian Wars, the War of 1812, the Great Rebellion; the Kansas problem and the California problem, the Indian question, and the Chinese question, Romanism and Communism, Eastern conservatism and Western

radicalism, the freedmen and the emigrant, State
rights and national sovereignty—all are the subordin-
ate factors whose harmonizing, reconciling, assimilating
factor is the divine purpose and plan in our History.
My friends, the Republic has a divine destiny to fulfil.
The Great Pilot is steering the ship of state for her
true haven. Scylla threatens on one side, Charybdis
on the other; but He knows the channel. The stormy
Euroclydon may strike her, tear her sails to tatters and
snap her ropes like burnt tow, and splinter her masts
to fragments; but He holds the winds in his fists.
Let us not fear. We have only to love, trust and obey
the God of our Fathers and He will guide us safely
and surely through all darkness and danger. The sins
that reproach our people are the only foes we have to
fear; the righteousness that exalts a nation the only
ally we need to covet. If the people of Michigan
would rear a grand monument to the heroic men who
have adorned our history, let us be true to the princi-
ples which they have defended, and to the God who
gave them to us as His instruments.

The DORIC PILLAR OF MICHIGAN has fallen; but
the State stands, and God can set another pillar in its
place. There is stone in the quarry—columns are
taking shape to-day in our homes and schools and
churches; and in God's time they shall be raised to
their place. Let us only be sure that in the shrine of

our nation God finds a throne, and not the idols of
this world, and not even the earthquake shock shall
shatter the symmetric structure of the Republic.